Real Science-4

Level I

Laboratory Workbook

Rebecca W. Keller, Ph.D.

Illustrations: Rebecca W. Keller, Ph.D.

Real Science-4-Kids: Physics Level I Laboratory Workbook

ISBN 978-1-936114184

Published by Gravitas Publications, Inc.
4116 Jackie Road SE, Suite 101
Rio Rancho, NM 87124
www.gravitaspublications.com

Gravitas
Publications Inc.

Keeping a laboratory notebook

A laboratory notebook is essential for the experimental scientist. In this type of notebook, the results of all the experiments are kept together along with comments and any additional information that is gathered. For this curriculum, you should use this workbook as your laboratory notebook and record your experimental observations and conclusions directly on its pages, just as a real scientist would.

The experimental section for each chapter is pre-written. The exact format of a notebook may vary among scientists, but all experiments written in a laboratory notebook have certain essential parts. For each experiment, a descriptive but short *Title* is written at the top of the page along with the *Date* the experiment is performed. Below the title, an *Objective* and a *Hypothesis* are written. The objective is a short statement that tells something about why you are doing the experiment, and the hypothesis is the predicted outcome. Next, a *Materials List* is written. The materials should be gathered before the experiment is started.

Following the Materials List, the *Experiment* is written. The sequence of steps for the experiment is written beforehand, and any changes should be noted during the experiment. All of the details of the experiment are written in this section. All information that might be of some importance is included. For example, if you are to measure 1 cup of water for an experiment, but you actually measured 1 1/4 cup, this should be recorded. It is hard sometimes to predict the way in which even small variations in an experiment will affect the outcome, and it is easier to track a problem if all of the information is recorded.

The next section is the *Results* section. Here you will record your experimental observations. It is extremely important that you be honest about what is observed. For example, if the experimental instructions say that a solution will turn yellow, but your solution turned blue, you must record blue. You may have done the experiment incorrectly, or you might have discovered a new and interesting result, but either way, it is very important that your observations be honestly recorded.

Finally, the *Conclusions* should be written. Here you will explain what the observations may mean. You should try to write only *valid* conclusions. It is important to learn to think about what the data actually show and what cannot be concluded from the experiment.

Contents

Experiment 1: Constellations

Date: _____

Objective _____

_____

Hypothesis _____

_____

Materials

student notebook
pencil
flashlight

Results

❶ In the evening on a clear night go outside and, without using a compass, locate "north." To do this you will need to find the Big Dipper. The Big Dipper is a set of stars that form the shape of a "dipping spoon." (The Big Dipper is not an official constellation but is called an asterism—a small group of stars.) The two stars on the end of the dipping spoon point to the star Polaris.

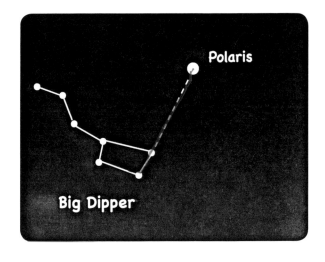

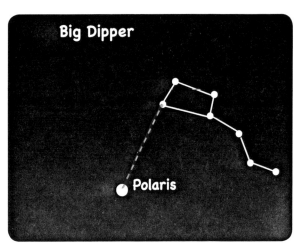

Polaris is the "North Star," and when you turn towards Polaris, you are pointing "north." It doesn't matter in which direction the Big Dipper is pointing, the two end stars always point to the North Star. The North Star is the only star in the sky that doesn't move (much). All of the constellations appear to move around the North Star. Once you find the North Star you can find nearby constellations.

❷   Now that you have found the North Star, try to find the constellation called the "Little Dipper."

Polaris forms the end of the handle of the Little Dipper.

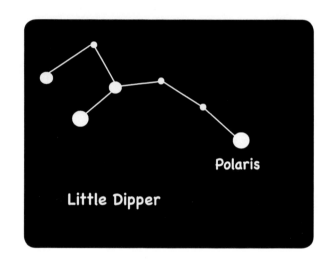

Draw the Little Dipper constellation as you observe it.

❸ Try to locate the "Dragon." The Dragon constellation is between the Big Dipper and Little Dipper.

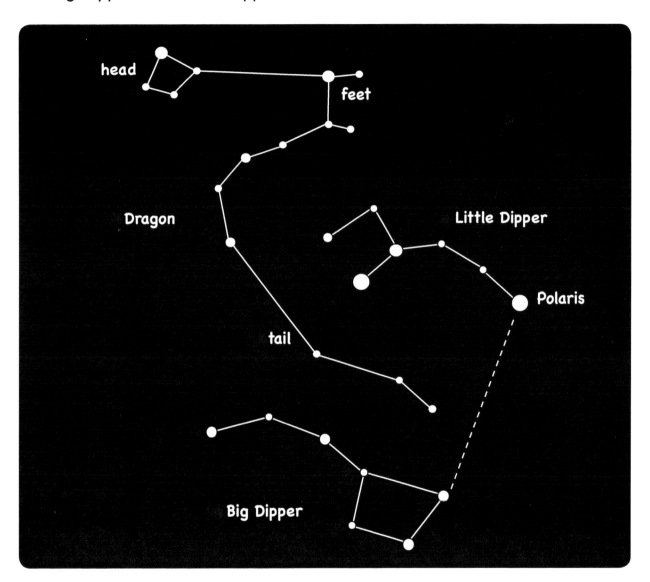

❹ On the following page, draw the Dragon constellation as you see it.

❺ Count the stars in the Dragon constellation in the image above. Compare this number with the number of stars you've recorded for the Dragon.

❻ Record your physical location, city, state, or country, whether you are in the Northern or Southern Hemisphere, and the month.

Location _____

_____

Hemisphere _____

Month _____

Conclusions

Summarize how easy or difficult it was to find the North Star, the Big Dipper asterism, and the two constellations—the Little Dipper and the Dragon. What role, if any, does your physical location and the month you made these observations have on your results?

_____

_____

_____

_____

_____

_____

_____

_____

_____

_____

_____

_____

Review

Answer the following:

1. The word astronomy comes from the Greek word _____ which means _____ and the Greek word _____ which means _____.

2. The word astronomy means _____.

3. The word geocentric comes from the Greek word _____ which means _____ and the Greek word _____ which means _____.

4. The word geocentric means _____.

5. The word heliocentric comes from the Greek word _____ which means _____ and the Greek word _____ which means _____.

6. The word heliocentric means _____.

7. A constellation is _____
   _____.

8. The North Star is also called _____.

Experiment 2: Measuring distances   Date: _____

Objective   _____

_____

Hypothesis   _____

_____

Materials

two sticks (used for marking)
two rulers
string
protractor
pencil
square grid or graph paper

Experiment

In this experiment you will use a simple triangulation method to measure the distance of a far away object.

❶ Find a wide open space with a distant object. The space can be a field, a city street, or even your own backyard.

❷ Pick two observation points and place the sticks at these points. Mark one observation point "A" and the other "B."

❸ Take the two rulers and connect them at one end making a right angle.

❹ Place the corner of the double ruler on observation point "A" with one end pointing towards the object you want to measure and the other end pointing towards observation point "B."

❺ Attach the string to the stick at observation point "A," and stretch it out along the side of the double ruler pointing towards observation point "B." The string will be used as a guide so that you walk in a straight line.

❻ Holding the string, walk toe-to-toe from observation point "A" to observation point "B" making sure the string is still pointing at a 90 degree angle in the direction of point "B." Count your steps.

❼ When you get to point "B," attach the string to the stick. Check to make sure the string is still pointing in the same direction as the ruler.

❽ From observation point "B" find the object whose distance you want to measure. Place the protractor on the string so that you can measure the angle between point "B" and the distant object.

❾ Record the angle between point "B" and the distant object, and record the number of steps between point "A" and point "B."

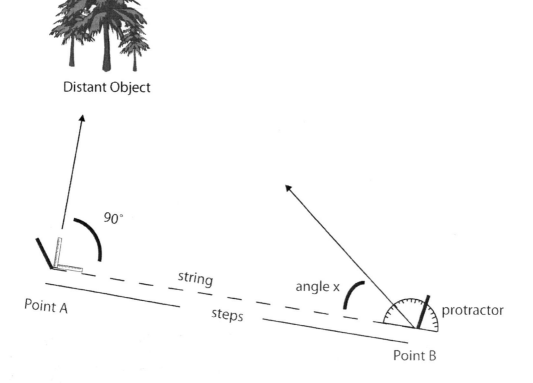

Distant Object

Results

❶ You will use graph paper and a modeling technique to measure the distance of the object.

❷ Take the square grid paper and mark point "A."

❸ Using one square for each step, find point "B" on the grid.

❹ Draw a line from point "A" to point "B." This is line AB.

❺ Draw a line from point "A" towards the distant object. This line should be at a 90 degree angle to line AB. Label this line "y."

❻ Using your protractor make a line from point "B" to the distant object using the angle you measured. Extend this line until it intersects with line "y." (You may have to extend line "y" in order for the two lines to intersect.)

❼ Count the number of squares from point "A" along line "y" to the distant object.

❽ Assuming that each of your steps is one foot, how far away is the distant object? Record your answers below.

Number of steps—point A to point B _____

Angle at point B _____

Number of squares—point A to distant object _____

Distance of object in feet _____

Conclusions

Summarize how easy or difficult it was to measure the distance of a far away object. Write down any problems or sources of error you might have noticed.

_____

_____

_____

_____

_____

_____

_____

_____

_____

_____

_____

Review

Answer the following:

1. The three types of telescopes are:

   _____

   _____

   _____

2. The largest refracting telescope ever constructed was:

   _____

   _____

3. Isaac Newton invented the _____ telescope, which is a type of _____ telescope.

2. Atmospheric turbulence causes _____

   _____

   _____

   _____

3. List three types of space probes scientists use to explore space.

   _____

   _____

   _____

Experiment 3: Lunar and Solar Eclipses   Date: _____

Objective   _____

_____

Hypothesis   _____

_____

Materials

basketball
ping-pong ball
flashlight
empty toilet paper tube
tape
scissors
a dark room

Experiment

❶ In this experiment you will observe the difference between lunar and solar eclipses.

❷ In a dark room, place the basketball on top of one end of a toilet paper tube that is sitting upright on the floor. The toilet paper tube will hold the basketball in place.

❸ With the flashlight, walk several feet away from the basketball. Turn on the flashlight, and point it towards the basketball. While keeping the basketball illuminated, lay the flashlight on the floor.

❹ Holding the ping-pong ball, adjust it so that the ping-pong ball is between the flashlight and the illuminated basketball. Note the shadow that is cast on the basketball.

❺   Move the ping-pong ball up until there is no shadow on the basketball.

❻   Now lower the ping-pong ball until there is no shadow on the basketball.

❼   Move the ping-pong ball in an "orbit" around the basketball. Observe where the ping-pong ball needs to be in order for the basketball to cast a shadow on the ping-pong ball.

❽   In the Results section, draw several of the "orbits" that you are testing, and note whether or not the ping-pong ball casts a shadow on the basketball or the basketball casts a shadow on the ping-pong ball (see the example below). You will need to spend some time "playing" with the ping-pong ball to observe where shadows occur.

Results

Example

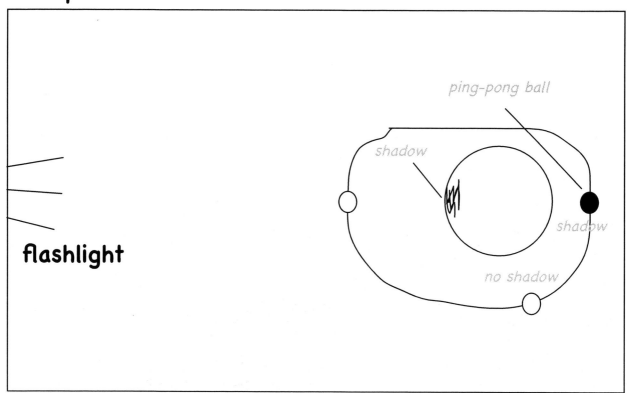

Conclusions

Based on your observations, discuss how a lunar eclipse occurs.

_____

_____

_____

_____

_____

_____

_____

Based on your observations, explain how a solar eclipse occurs.

_____

_____

_____

_____

_____

Review

Answer the following:

1. The word planet comes from the Greek word _____ which means _____.

2. To qualify as a planet, a celestial body must meet the following criteria:

    _____

    _____

    _____

    _____

3. Define orbital obliquity and explain why this gives us seasons.

    _____

    _____

    _____

    _____

4. The word moon comes from the Greek word _____ which means _____. The Moon completes an orbit of the Earth every _____ days.

5. A lunar eclipse occurs when _____

    _____

6. A solar eclipse occurs when _____

    _____

Experiment 4: Modeling the Moon   Date: _____

Objective   _____

_____

Hypothesis   _____

_____

Materials

Modeling clay with the following colors:
    gray
    white
    brown
    red
butter knife or sculptor's knife
ruler

Experiment

❶   Model building is an important part of science. Models help scientists visualize how something might look in three dimensions.

❷   Observe the image of the Moon on page 27 of your student textbook. Note the colors of the core, mantle and crust of the Moon.

❸   Using the modeling clay, build a model that resembles the image in your student textbook. Note any color variations on the surface, and try to duplicate the image with your model.

❹   Measure the diameter of your model Moon with a ruler.

Results

The real Moon is 2158 miles in diameter. Compare the diameter of your model with the actual diameter of the Moon. Do the following steps to calculate how many times smaller your model is compared to the actual size of the Moon.

❶ Write the diameter of your model Moon in inches _____ or in centimeters _____. The diameter of the actual Moon is 2158 miles (3478.8 kilometers).

❷ Convert the diameter of your model Moon to kilometers.

If you are using inches, first multiply by 2.54 to get centimeters.

_____ inches X 2.54 = _____ centimeters.

Multiply the number of centimeters by 0.001 to get kilometers. This will be a very small number.

_____ centimeters X 0.001 = _____ kilometers.

❸ Divide the actual diameter of the Moon by the diameter of your model Moon.

3478.8 kilometers (actual Moon) ÷ _____ kilometers (model Moon) = _____.

This should be a very large number. It tells you how many times larger the real Moon is compared to your model Moon.

Conclusions

How easy or difficult was it to build a model of the Moon?

_____

_____

_____

_____

_____

_____

_____

Based on your calculation, how much larger is the actual Moon compared to your model Moon? What does this mean to you?

_____

_____

_____

_____

Review

Answer the following:

1. The word lunar comes from the Greek word _____ which means
   _____.

2. The two types of rocks that have been found on the Moon are:

   _____

   _____

3. Explain why the Moon has less gravity than Earth.

   _____

   _____

   _____

   _____

4. The dark areas of the Moon are called _____ meaning _____.

5. The light areas of the Moon are called _____ meaning _____.

6. Like Earth, the Moon has a _____, _____, and _____..

7. Unlike Earth, the Moon has no _____ or _____.

8. The Sun is made of two gases: _____ and _____.

9. The Sun is about _____ times the diameter of Earth.

10. The Sun generates energy through a process called _____.

Experiment 5: Modeling the Planets   Date: _____

Objective   _____

_____

Hypothesis   _____

_____

Materials

Modeling clay with the following colors:
gray
white
brown
red
blue
green
orange
butter knife or sculptor's knife
ruler

Experiment

❶   In this experiment you will model the eight planets of the solar system.

❷   Look closely at the images of the eight planets in Chapter 5 of your student textbook. Observe their relative sizes (which planets are larger or smaller than the others), and their shape and colors.

❸   In the space below write notes about what you can observe from the student textbook images. Also make a quick sketch of each planet, noting any important features (such as rings or spots). You will use these notes as a guide for your models.

Mercury

_____

_____

_____

_____

Venus

_____

_____

_____

_____

Earth

_____

_____

_____

_____

Mars

_____

_____

_____

_____

Jupiter

_____

_____

_____

_____

Saturn

_____

_____

_____

_____

Uranus

_____

_____

_____

_____

Neptune

_____

_____

_____

_____

❹   Using the modeling clay, create a model of each planet. Make sure that you keep the relative sizes in proportion (Jupiter is larger than Earth, Mercury is smaller than Venus, and so on).

Results

Observe the model planets you have created. Are they the correct relative size? Do they match the images in the book? Are they all spherical in shape? Record your observations below:

_____

_____

_____

_____

_____

_____

_____

_____

_____

_____

_____

_____

Conclusions

How easy or difficult was it to build the models of the planets?

_____

_____

_____

_____

_____

_____

_____

Discuss how well your models do or do not represent the real planets.

_____

_____

_____

_____

_____

Review

Answer the following:

1. List the eight planets of the solar system, from closest to farthest from the Sun.

   _____

   _____

   _____

   _____

   _____

   _____

   _____

   _____

2. The word terrestrial comes from the Latin word _____
   which means _____.

3. List the four terrestrial planets.

   _____

   _____

   _____

   _____

3. The term Jovian comes from _____.

4. List the four Jovian planets.

   _____

   _____

   _____

   _____

Experiment 6: Modeling the Solar System Date: _____

Objective _____

_____

Hypothesis _____

_____

Materials

the eight planet models from Experiment 5
ruler (in centimeters)
pencil
large flat surface for drawing—3 x 3 feet (You can use a large piece
    of cardboard or several sheets of construction paper.)
large open space at least 10 feet long
push pin
piece of string a meter long

Experiment

❶ In this experiment you will model the planetary orbits of the solar system.

❷ Take the cardboard and mark the center with a pen.

❸ Using the push pin, fix the string to the center mark of the cardboard.

❹ Wrap the free end of the string around the pencil. Position the pencil 10 centimeters from the center mark, pull the string tight, and with the pencil touching the cardboard, draw a circle around the center mark. This is the orbital path for Earth.

❺ Draw concentric circles for the first five planetary orbits (Mercury through Jupiter) using the distances listed below. You will need to adjust the length of the string for each orbit. Place the models of the planets you created in Experiment 5 at their corresponding orbit distance from the center.

Planet	Distance from center
Mercury	4 cm
Venus	7 cm
Earth	10 cm
Mars	15 cm
Jupiter	50 cm
Saturn	90 cm (3 ft)
Uranus	190 cm (6 ft)
Neptune	300 cm (10 ft)

❻ For the last three orbits, walk to the correct distance away from the center. Place the planetary model you created in Experiment 5 at the appropriate distance.

Results

Observe your model of the solar system, and compare your model with the illustration on page 45 of your student textbook. On the following page, note any similarities or differences between your model of the solar system and the illustration.

Similarities

_____

_____

_____

_____

_____

_____

_____

_____

Differences

_____

_____

_____

_____

_____

_____

_____

_____

Conclusions

How easy or difficult was it to create a model of the solar system? How did the different distances affect how you could build your model?

_____

_____

_____

_____

Review

Answer the following:

1. The four terrestrial planets that make up the inner solar system are:

   _____

   _____

   _____

   _____

2. The four Jovian planets that make up the outer solar system are:

   _____

   _____

   _____

   _____

3. Define a planetary orbit.

   _____.

4. The orbits of the planets are nearly circular, but because they are not perfectly circular, they are called _____.

5. The gap between the inner and outer planets is filled with _____

   _____.

4. Why is Earth habitable but the other planets are not?

   _____

   _____

   _____

Experiment 7: Designing Life on Other Planets

Date: _____

Thought Experiment

Sometimes it's not possible to do an actual experiment, and yet it can be very useful to do what is called a "thought experiment." A thought experiment is a mental exercise in which an experiment is simply imagined. The process of imagining how a hypothesis might be explored or how an experiment might actually work is very valuable to science. Albert Einstein wondered what it would be like to ride on a rainbow. He could not literally ride on a rainbow, but he could imagine it, and the ideas he generated during this thought experiment helped him discover the theory of relativity.

Materials

    pen
    paper
    your imagination

Experiment

❶ Imagine that you are traveling at the outer edges of our solar system and you come across a star three times the size of our Sun. You observe ten planets in the solar system around this sun. Some of the planets have moons. Assume that you can travel to all ten planets and explore all of their moons.

❷ Do a thought experiment and write in as much detail as possible what you would need to do to locate life on any of the ten planets or moons. Imagine this is really possible. Think about what you would need to take and how you would define "life." Also consider which planets are more likely to have life and which you can ignore.

Finding life

_____

_____

_____

_____

_____

_____

_____

_____

_____

_____

_____

_____

_____

_____

_____

_____

_____

_____

_____

_____

_____

_____

_____

_____

_____

_____

_____

_____

_____

_____

_____

_____

Review

Answer the following:

1. The three stars that are closest to our solar system are part of a triple-star system called the _____.

   The three stars in this system are:

   _____

   _____

   _____

2. A parsec is _____ AUs.

3. The brightest star in the sky is called _____.

4. The largest star in the sky is called _____.

5. An exoplanet is a planet that:

   _____

   _____

   _____

6. Define the Circumstellar Habitable Zone.

   _____

   _____

   _____

   _____

   _____

Experiment 8: The Center of the Milky Way   Date: _____

Objective

_____

_____

Hypothesis

_____

_____

Materials

pen
paper
computer and internet service
Google Earth

Experiment

❶   Set up Google Earth on your computer.

①   Go to http://earth.google.com and click "Download Google Earth."

②   Click "Agree and Download."

③   Once the file has been downloaded, install the program.

④   Open the Google Earth program on your computer.

⑤   Set up Google Earth in Sky Mode.

⑥   At the top, click "View" and then click "Switch to Sky."

⑦   On the left-hand side of the window, you should see "Layers."

⑧   Uncheck every item except "Imagery" and "Backyard Astronomy."

⑨   Click the arrow next to "Backyard Astronomy."

⑩   Uncheck every item except "Constellations."

❷   The Appendix at the back of this book gives data for globular clusters observed in our Milky Way Galaxy. The data table shows 158 globular clusters compiled as of June 30, 2010. From left to right the table lists the ID, name, and cross-reference for the cluster followed by the constellation where the cluster is located and various astronomical parameters associated with the cluster.

❸   Look at the data table in the Appendix, and locate the three constellations that have the highest number of globular clusters. [Note: The number of globular clusters observed in a constellation is found in parentheses next to the constellation name. Constellations with fewer than two globular clusters are not listed.]

❹   Write the three constellations with the highest number of globular clusters below.

Constellation Name	# of Globular Clusters

Results

❶   Open Google Earth and toggle the "sky" button so that you are looking at the sky. In the "Search the Sky" button, type in the name of one of the three constellations you listed above. Adjust the view so that you see all three constellations. This location should be the center of the Milky Way Galaxy.

❷   Type in "Galactic Center" to check your results.

Conclusions

Based on your observations, where is the galactic center of the Milky Way? How easy or difficult do you think it is to find the center of a galaxy?

_____

_____

_____

_____

_____

_____

_____

_____

_____

_____

_____

_____

_____

Review

Answer the following:

1. Write a definition of galaxy.

   _____

   _____

   _____

2. What are the three basic categories of galaxies?

   _____

   _____

   _____

3. What type of galaxy is the Milky Way? _____

4. List the names of the two major spiral arms and two minor spiral arms of the Milky Way galaxy.

   _____   _____

   _____   _____

5. Define the galactic habitable zone.

   _____

   _____

   _____

   _____

Experiment 9: Finding Galaxies   Date: ____

Objective

_____

_____

Hypothesis

_____

_____

Materials

pen
paper
computer and internet service
Google Earth

Experiment

❶ Open the Google Earth program on your computer.

(If you have not yet set up Google Earth on your computer, see the instructions in Experiment 8.)

① At the top, click "View" and then click "Switch to Sky," or click on the planet symbol.

② On the left-hand side of the window, you should see "Layers."

③ Uncheck every item, except "Imagery" and "Backyard Astronomy."

④ Click the arrow next to "Backyard Astronomy."

⑤ Uncheck every item except "Constellations."

❷ Using Google Earth, do a search for the galaxies listed in the following table. Categorize each galaxy as either spiral, elliptical, or irregular

Name	Type
Whirlpool Galaxy	
NGC 1427A	
M 101	
M 82	
Bode's Galaxy	
M 87	
Sombrero Galaxy	
Sunflower Galaxy	
Hoag's Object	
Cartwheel Galaxy	
NGC 3314	

Results

❶ Look for two galaxies that are not named.

❷ Draw each below, give the location, assign a name, and list the type.

location

_____

name

_____

type

_____

location

_____

name

_____

type

_____

Conclusions

Based on your observations, how easy or difficult is it to identify galaxies and categorize them? What else did you discover about galaxies?

_____

_____

_____

_____

_____

_____

_____

_____

_____

_____

_____

_____

_____

_____

Review

Answer the following:

1. What is the name and type of our closest galactic neighbor?

_____

_____

_____

2. What is the difference between a barred spiral galaxy and a spiral galaxy? Draw each below.

_____

_____

3. What is the difference between elliptical galaxies and irregular galaxies?

_____

_____

_____

_____

Experiment 10: Searching for Nebulae   Date: _____

Objective

_____

_____

Hypothesis

_____

_____

Materials

pen
paper
computer and internet service
Google Earth

Experiment

❶ Open the Google Earth program on your computer.

(If you have not yet set up Google Earth on your computer, see the instructions in Experiment 8.)

① At the top, click "View," and then click "Switch to Sky."

② On the left-hand side of the window, you should see "Layers."

③ Uncheck every item, except "Imagery" and "Backyard Astronomy."

④ Click the arrow next to "Backyard Astronomy."

⑤ Uncheck every item except "Constellations."

❷ Using Google Earth, search for the following nebulae. Illustrate what you observe, and note the location of each nebula by naming any nearby constellations.

Helix Nebula

location
_____
_____

Cat's Eye Nebula

location
_____
_____

Crab Nebula

location
_____
_____

Eagle Nebula

location
_____
_____

Cone Nebula

location
_____
_____

Orion Nebula

location
_____
_____

❸ Using Google Earth, scan the sky by moving the window left and right, up and down, zooming in and zooming out.

❹ Search for a black hole. Draw what you observe. Also search for any other objects you find interesting, and label them star, galaxy, nebula, or black hole.

<table>
<tr><td></td><td>location
_____
_____

type
_____
_____</td><td></td><td>location
_____
_____

type
_____
_____</td></tr>
<tr><td></td><td>location
_____
_____

type
_____
_____</td><td></td><td>location
_____
_____

type
_____
_____</td></tr>
</table>

Results

Describe what you discovered.

_____

_____

_____

_____

_____

Conclusions

How easy or difficult is it to identify nebulae or other features in the sky? Do you think all of the galaxies, stars, and nebulae in the universe have been discovered? Why or why not?

_____

_____

_____

_____

_____

_____

_____

_____

_____

_____

_____

_____

_____

_____

Review

Answer the following:

1. What is a red giant star?

_____

_____

2. What is white dwarf star?

_____

_____

3. What happens to a star that has become a nova or supernova?

_____

_____

_____

_____

4. Knowing that the center of the Milky Way Galaxy is full of stars, do you think that when you are looking for objects in the sky, such as nebulae, it is an advantage that Earth is located on an outside spiral arm of the galaxy? Why or why not?

_____

_____

_____

_____

Appendix: Globular Clusters

On the following pages are several data tables with information about globular clusters observed in the Milky Way. Learning how to read data tables and sorting through the information that is needed for an experiment is an important part of scientific investigation.

Key

M, NGC/IC, ID/Name/Crossref:

Messier number, NGC or IC number, and other identification or name

Con:

Constellation name (number of globular clusters)

RA, Dec (2000):

Right Ascension and Declination for epoch 2000.0

R_Sun, R_gc:

Distance from our Sun and the Galactic Center in thousands of light years (kly)

m_v:

Apparent visual magnitude

dim:

Apparent dimension in arc minutes

M	NGC/IC	ID/Name/Crossref	Con	RA (2000)	DEC	R_Sun	R_gc	m_v	dim
	104	47 Tuc Lac l.1	Tucana (2)	00:24:05.2	-72:04:51	14.7	24.1	3.95	50.0
	288	H 6.20	Scl	00:52:47.5	-26:35:24	28.7	39.1	8.09	13.0
	362	Dun 62	Tucana (2)	01:03:14.3	-70:50:54	27.7	30.3	6.40	14.0
		Whiting 1	Cet	02:02:56.8	-03:15:10				1.2
	1261	Dun 337	Horologium (2)	03:12:15.3	-55:13:01	53.5	59.4	8.29	6.6
		Pal 1	Cep	03:33:23.0	+79:34:50	35.6	55.4	13.18	2.8
		AM 1 E 1	Horologium (2)	03:55:02.7	-49:36:52	397.6	401.8	15.72	0.5
		Eri	Eri	04:24:44.5	-21:11:13	294.2	310.5	14.70	1.0
		Pal 2	Aur	04:46:05.9	+31:22:51	90.0	115.5	13.04	2.2
	1851	Dun 508	Col	05:14:06.3	-40:02:50	39.5	54.5	7.14	12.0
M 79	1904		Lep	05:24:10.6	-24:31:27	42.1	61.3	7.73	9.6
	2298	Dun 578	Pup	06:48:59.2	-36:00:19	34.9	51.2	9.29	5.0
	2419	H 1.218	Lyn	07:38:08.5	+38:52:55	274.6	298.4	10.39	4.6
		Koposov 2	Gem	07:58:17.0	+26:15:18	130			
		Pyxisis	Pyx	09:07:57.8	-37:13:17	129.4	135.9	12.90	4.0
	2808	Dun 265	Car	09:12:02.6	-64:51:47	31.2	36.2	6.20	14.0
		E 3	Cha	09:20:59.3	-77:16:57	14.0	24.8	11.35	10:
		Pal 3	Sex	10:05:31.4	+00:04:17	302.3	312.8	14.26	1.6
		Segue 1	Leo	10:07:04	+12:47:30	75.0	14.7	4.5	
	3201	Dun 445	Vel	10:17:36.8	-46:24:40	16.3	29.0	6.75	20.0
		Pal 4	UMa	11:29:16.8	+28:58:25	356.2	364.6	14.20	1.3
		Koposov 1	Virgo (2)	11:59:18.5	+12:15:36	160			
	4147	H 1.19	Coma Berenices (3)	12:10:06.2	+18:32:31	62.9	69.5	10.32	4.4
	4372		Mus	12:25:45.4	-72:39:33	18.9	23.2	7.24	5.0
		Rup 106	Cen	12:38:40.2	-51:09:01	69.1	60.3	10.90	2.0
M 68	4590		Hya	12:39:28.0	-26:44:34	33.3	32.9	7.84	11.0
	4833	Lac l.4 Dun 164	Mus	12:59:35.0	-70:52:29	21.2	22.8	6.91	14.0
M 53	5024		Coma Berenices (3)	13:12:55.3	+18:10:09	58.0	59.6	7.61	13.0
	5053	H 6.7	Coma Berenices (3)	13:16:27.0	+17:41:53	53.5	55.1	9.47	10.0
	5139	Omega Cen Lac l.5	Cen	13:26:45.9	-47:28:37	17.3	20.9	3.68	55.0
M 3	5272		CVn	13:42:11.2	+28:22:32	33.9	39.8	6.19	18.0
	5286	Dun 388	Cen	13:46:26.5	-51:22:24	35.9	27.4	7.34	11.0
		AM 4	Hya	13:56:21.2	-27:10:04	97.5	83.2	15.90	3.0
	5466	H 6.9	Boo	14:05:27.3	+28:32:04	51.8	52.8	9.04	9.0
	5634	H 1.70	Virgo (2)	14:29:37.3	-05:58:35	82.2	69.1	9.47	5.5
	5694	H 2.196	Hya	14:39:36.5	-26:32:18	113.2	94.9	10.17	4.3

		I4499	Aps	15:00:18.5	-82:12:49	61.6	51.2	9.76	8.0
	5824		Lup	15:03:58.5	-33:04:04	104.4	84.1	9.09	7.4
		Pal 5	SerCp	15:16:05.3	-00:06:41	75.7	60.7	11.75	8.0
	5897	H 6.8 H 6.19	Lib	15:17:24.5	-21:00:37	40.4	23.8	8.53	11.0
M 5	5904		SerCp	15:18:33.8	+02:04:58	24.5	20.2	5.65	23.0
	5927	Dun 389	Lup	15:28:00.5	-50:40:22	24.8	14.7	8.01	6.0
	5946		Norma (3)	15:35:28.5	-50:39:34	34.6	18.9	9.61	3.0
		BH 176	Norma (3)	15:39:07.3	-50:03:02	50.9	31.6	14.00	3.0
	5986	Dun 552	Lup	15:46:03.5	-37:47:10	33.9	15.7	7.52	9.6
		Lynga 7	Norma (3)	16:11:03.0	-55:18:52	23.5	2.5		
		Pal 14 AvdB	Her	16:11:04.9	+14:57:29	241.0	225.0	14.74	2.5
M 80	6093		Scorpio (20)	16:17:02.5	-22:58:30	32.6	12.4	7.33	10.0
M 4	6121	Lac I.9	Scorpio (20)	16:23:35.5	-26:31:31	7.2	19.2	5.63	36.0
	6101	Dun 68	Aps	16:25:48.6	-72:12:06	49.9	36.2	9.16	5.0
	6144	H 6.10	Scorpio (20)	16:27:14.1	-26:01:29	27.7	8.5	9.01	7.4
	6139	Dun 536	Scorpio (20)	16:27:40.4	-38:50:56	32.9	11.7	8.99	8.2
		Terzan 3	Scorpio (20)	16:28:40.1	-35:21:13	24.5	7.8	12.00	3.0
M 107	6171	H 6.40	Ophiuchus (25)	16:32:31.9	-13:03:13	20.9	10.8	7.93	13.0
		1636-283 ESO452-SC11	Scorpio (20)	16:39:25.5	-28:23:52	25.4	6.5	12.00	1.2
M 13	6205		Her	16:41:41.5	+36:27:37	25.1	28.4	5.78	20.0
	6229	H 4.50	Her	16:46:58.9	+47:31:40	99.1	96.8	9.39	4.5
M 12	6218		Ophiuchus (25)	16:47:14.5	-01:56:52	16.0	14.7	6.70	16.0
		FSR 1735 2MASS-GC03	Arae (5)	16:52:10.6	-47:03:29	29.7	10.4	0.8	
	6235	H 2.584	Ophiuchus (25)	16:53:25.4	-22:10:38	37.2	13.4	9.97	5.0
M 10	6254		Ophiuchus (25)	16:57:08.9	-04:05:58	14.4	15.0	6.60	20.0
	6256		Scorpio (20)	16:59:32.6	-37:07:17	27.4	5.9	11.29	4.1
		Pal 15	Ophiuchus (25)	17:00:02.4	-00:32:31	145.5	123.6	14.00	3.0
M 62	6266	Dun 627	Ophiuchus (25)	17:01:12.6	-30:06:44	22.5	5.5	6.45	15.0
M 19	6273		Ophiuchus (25)	17:02:37.7	-26:16:05	28.0	5.2	6.77	17.0
	6284	H 6.11	Ophiuchus (25)	17:04:28.8	-24:45:53	49.9	24.8	8.83	6.2
	6287	H 2.195	Ophiuchus (25)	17:05:09.4	-22:42:29	30.3	6.8	9.35	4.8
	6293	H 6.12	Ophiuchus (25)	17:10:10.4	-26:34:54	28.7	4.6	8.22	8.2
	6304	H 1.147	Ophiuchus (25)	17:14:32.5	-29:27:44	19.6	7.2	8.22	8.0
	6316	H 1.45	Ophiuchus (25)	17:16:37.4	-28:08:24	35.9	10.4	8.43	5.4
M 92	6341		Her	17:17:07.3	+43:08:11	26.7	31.3	6.44	14.0
	6325		Ophiuchus (25)	17:17:59.2	-23:45:57	26.1	3.6	10.33	4.1
M 9	6333		Ophiuchus (25)	17:19:11.8	-18:30:59	25.8	5.5	7.72	12.0
	6342	H 1.149	Ophiuchus (25)	17:21:10.2	-19:35:14	28.0	5.5	9.66	4.4
	6356	H 1.48	Ophiuchus (25)	17:23:35.0	-17:48:47	49.6	24.8	8.25	10.0

M	NGC	Name	Constellation	RA	Dec					
	6355	H 1.46	Ophiuchus (25)	17:23:58.6	-26:21:13	31.0	5.9		9.14	4.2
	6352	Dun 417	Arae (5)	17:25:29.2	-48:25:22	18.6	10.8		7.96	9.0
		I1257	Ophiuchus (25)	17:27:08.5	-07:05:35	81.5	58.4		13.10	5.0
		Terzan 2 HP 3	Scorpio (20)	17:27:33.4	-30:48:08	28.4	2.9		14.29	0.6
	6366		Ophiuchus (25)	17:27:44.3	-05:04:36	11.7	16.3		9.20	13.0
		Terzan 4 HP 4	Scorpio (20)	17:30:38.9	-31:35:44	29.7	4.2		16.00	0.7
		HP 1 BH 229	Ophiuchus (25)	17:31:05.2	-29:58:54	46.0	19.9		11.59	1.2
	6362	Dun 225	Arae (5)	17:31:54.8	-67:02:53	24.8	16.6		7.73	15.0
		Liller 1	Scorpio (20)	17:33:24.5	-33:23:20	34.2	8.5		16.77	12.6
	6380	Ton 1	Scorpio (20)	17:34:28.0	-39:04:09	34.9	10.4		11.31	3.6
		FSR 1767	Scorpio (20)	17:35:43	-36:21:28	4.9	18.6			
		Terzan 1 HP 2	Scorpio (20)	17:35:47.8	-30:28:11	18.3	8.2		15.90	2.4
		Ton 2 Pismis 26	Scorpio (20)	17:36:10.5	-38:33:12	26.4	4.6		12.24	2.2
	6388	Dun 457	Scorpio (20)	17:36:17.0	-44:44:06	32.6	10.4		6.72	10.4
M 14	6402	H 1.44	Ophiuchus (25)	17:37:36.1	-03:14:45	30.3	13.4		7.59	11.0
	6401		Ophiuchus (25)	17:38:36.9	-23:54:32	34.2	8.8		9.45	4.8
	6397	Lac III.11 Dun 366	Arae (5)	17:40:41.3	-53:40:25	7.5	19.6		5.73	31.0
		Pal 6	Ophiuchus (25)	17:43:42.2	-26:13:21	19.2	7.2		11.55	1.2
	6426	H 2.587	Ophiuchus (25)	17:44:54.7	+03:10:13	67.5	47.6		11.01	4.2
		Djorg 1	Scorpio (20)	17:47:28.3	-33:03:56	39.1	13.4		13.60	
		Terzan 5 Terzan 11	Sagittarius (34)	17:48:04.9	-24:48:45	33.6	7.8		13.85	2.4
	6440	H 1.150	Sagittarius (34)	17:48:52.6	-20:21:34	27.4	4.2		9.20	4.4
	6441	Dun 557	Scorpio (20)	17:50:12.9	-37:03:04	38.1	12.7		7.15	9.6
		Terzan 6 HP 5	Scorpio (20)	17:50:46.4	-31:16:31	31.0	5.2		13.85	1.4
	6453		Scorpio (20)	17:50:51.8	-34:35:55	31.3	5.9	10.0	7.6	
		UKS 1 UKS 1751-241	Sagittarius (34)	17:54:27.2	-24:08:43	27.1	2.6		17.29	2.0
	6496	Dun 460	Scorpio (20)	17:59:02.0	-44:15:54	37.5	14.0		8.54	5.6
		Terzan 9	Sagittarius (34)	18:01:38.8	-26:50:23	21.2	5.2		16.00	0.2
		Djorg 2 E456-SC38	Sagittarius (34)	18:01:49.1	-27:49:33	21.9	4.6		9.90	9.9
	6517	H 2.199	Ophiuchus (25)	18:01:50.6	-08:57:32	35.2	14.0		10.23	4.0
		Terzan 10	Sagittarius (34)	18:02:57.4	-26:04:00	18.6	7.8		14.90	1.5
	6522	H 1.49	Sagittarius (34)	18:03:34.1	-30:02:02	25.4	2.0		8.27	9.4
	6535		SerCd	18:03:50.7	-00:17:49	22.2	12.7		10.47	3.4
	6528	H 2.200	Sagittarius (34)	18:04:49.6	-30:03:21	25.8	2.0		9.60	5.0
	6539		SerCd	18:04:49.8	-07:35:09	27.4	10.1		9.33	7.9
	6540	H 2.198 Djorg 3	Sagittarius (34)	18:06:08.6	-27:45:55	12.1	14.4		9.30	1.5
	6544	H 2.197	Sagittarius (34)	18:07:20.6	-24:59:51	8.8	17.3		7.77	9.2
	6541	Dun 473	CrA	18:08:02.2	-43:42:20	22.8	7.2		6.30	15.0
		2MASS-GC01	Sagittarius (34)	18:08:21.8	-19:49:47	11.7	14.7		3.3	

		ESO 280-SC06	Arae (5)	18:09:06	-46:25:24	70.7	46.6	1.5	
	6553	H 4.12	Sagittarius (34)	18:09:15.6	-25:54:28	19.6	7.2	8.06	9.2
		2MASS-GC02	Sagittarius (34)	18:09:36.5	-20:46:44	13.0	13.4	1.9	4.2
	6558		Sagittarius (34)	18:10:18.4	-31:45:49	24.1	3.3	9.26	8.0
		I1276 Pal 7	SerCd	18:10:44.2	-07:12:27	17.6	12.1	10.34	1.0
		Terzan 12	Sagittarius (34)	18:12:15.8	-22:44:31	15.7	11.1	15.63	6.4
	6569	H 2.201 Dun 619	Sagittarius (34)	18:13:38.9	-31:49:35	34.9	9.5	8.55	1.3
		AL 3	Sagittarius (34)	18:14:05.7	-28:38:08				
	6584	Dun 376	Tel	18:18:37.7	-52:12:54	43.7	22.8	8.27	6.6
	6624	H 1.50	Sagittarius (34)	18:23:40.5	-30:21:40	25.8	3.9	7.87	8.8
M 28	6626	Lac I.11	Sagittarius (34)	18:24:32.9	-24:52:12	18.3	8.8	6.79	11.2
	6638	H 1.51	Sagittarius (34)	18:30:56.2	-25:29:47	31.2	7.5	9.02	7.3 M, 6
	6637	Lac I.12 Dun 613	Sagittarius (34)	18:31:23.2	-32:20:53	29.7	6.2	7.64	9.8
	6642	H 2.205	Sagittarius (34)	18:31:54.3	-23:28:35	27.4	5.5	9.13	5.8
	6652		Sagittarius (34)	18:35:45.7	-32:59:25	32.9	9.1	8.62	6.0
M 22	6656		Sagittarius (34)	18:36:24.2	-23:54:12	10.4	16.0	5.10	32.0
		Pal 8	Sagittarius (34)	18:41:29.9	-19:49:33	42.1	18.3	11.02	5.2
M 70	6681	Dun 614	Sagittarius (34)	18:43:12.7	-32:17:31	29.4	6.8	7.87	8.0
		GLIMPSE-C01	Aquila (4)	18:48:49.7	-01:29:50			10-17	
	6712	H 1.47	Sct	18:53:04.3	-08:42:22	22.5	11.4	8.10	9.8
M 54	6715	Dun 624	Sagittarius (34)	18:55:03.3	-30:28:42	87.3	62.6	7.60	12.0
	6717	H 3.143 Pal 9	Sagittarius (34)	18:55:06.2	-22:42:03	23.1	7.8	9.28	5.4
	6723	Dun 573	Sagittarius (34)	18:59:33.2	-36:37:54	28.4	8.4	7.01	13.0
	6749	Berkeley 42	Aquila (4)	19:05:15.3	+01:54:03	25.8	16.3	12.44	4.0
	6752	Dun 295	Pav	19:10:51.8	-59:58:55	13.0	17.0	5.40	29.0
	6760		Aquila (4)	19:11:12.1	+01:01:50	24.1	15.7	8.88	9.6
M 56	6779		Lyr	19:16:35.5	+30:11:05	32.9	31.6	8.27	8.8
		Terzan 7	Sagittarius (34)	19:17:43.7	-34:39:27	75.7	52.2	12.00	1.2
		Pal 10	Sge	19:18:02.1	+18:34:18	19.2	20.9	13.22	4.0
		Arp 2	Sagittarius (34)	19:28:44.1	-30:21:14	93.3	69.8	12.30	2.3
M 55	6809	Lac I.14 Dun 620	Sagittarius (34)	19:39:59.4	-30:57:44	17.3	12.7	6.32	19.0
		Terzan 8	Sagittarius (34)	19:41:45.0	-34:00:01	84.8	62.3	12.40	3.5
		Pal 11	Aquila (4)	19:45:14.4	-08:00:26	42.4	25.8	9.80	10.0
M 71	6838		Sge	19:53:46.1	+18:46:42	13.0	21.9	8.19	7.2
M 75	6864		Sagittarius (34)	20:06:04.8	-21:55:17	67.5	47.6	8.52	6.8
	6934	H 1.103	Delphinus (2)	20:34:11.6	+07:24:15	51.2	41.7	8.83	7.1
M 72	6981		Aqr	20:53:27.9	-12:32:13	55.4	42.1	9.27	6.6
	7006	H 1.52	Delphinus (2)	21:01:29.5	+16:11:15	135.4	126.5	10.56	3.6
M 15	7078		Peg	21:29:58.3	+12:10:01	33.6	33.9	6.20	18.0

M 2	7089		Aqr	21:33:29.3	-00:49:23	37.5	33.9	6.47	16.0
M 30	7099		Cap	21:40:22.0	-23:10:45	26.1	23.2	7.19	12.0
		Pal 12 Cap Dwarf	Cap	21:46:38.8	-21:15:03	62.3	51.9	11.99	2.9
		Pal 13	Peg	23:06:44.4	+12:46:19	84.1	87.0	13.80	0.7
	7492	H 3.558	Aqr	23:08:26.7	-15:36:41	84.1	81.2	11.29	4.2

References

V. Berokurov, D.B. Zucker, N.W. Evans, J.T. Kleyna, S. Koposov, S.T. Hodgkin, M.J. Irwin, G. Gilmore, M.I. Wilkinson, M. Fellhauer, D.M. Bramich, P.C. Hewett, S. Vidrir, J.T.A. de Jong, J.A. Smith, H.-W. Rix, E.F. Bell, R.F.G. Wyse, H.J. Newberg, P.A. Mayeur, B. Yanny, C.M. Rockosi, O.Y. Gnedin, D.P. Schneider, T.C. Beers, J.C. Barentine, H. Brewington, J. Brinkmann, M. Harvanek, S.J. Kleinman, J. Krzesinski, D. Long, A. Nitta, S.A. Sneddon, 2007. Cats and Dogs, Hair and a Hero: A Quintet of New Milky Way Companions. Astrophysical Journal, Vol. 654, Issue 2, pp. 897-906 (January 2007) [ADS: 2007ApJ...654..897B] - [Preprint: astro-ph/0608448] Discovery announce of Segue 1.

C. Bonatto, E. Bica, S. Ortolani and B. Barbuy, 2007. FSR 1767 - a new globular cluster in the Galaxy. To be published in: Monthly Notices of the Royal Astronomical Society. [Preprint: arXiv:0708.0501[astro-ph]] Discovery announce of FSR-1767.

D. Froebrich, H. Meusinger and A. Scholz, 2007. SR 1735 - A new globular cluster candidate in the inner Galaxy. To appear in: Monthly Notices of the Royal Astronomical Society (2007). [Preprint: astro-ph/0703318] Discovery announce of FSR-1735.

W.E. Harris, 1996-1999. Catalog of Parameters for Milky Way Globular Clusters. AJ, 112, 1487. Revision of June 22, 1999. Available online; also see references and the potentially more current original site.

R.J. Hurt, et al., 2000. Serendipitous 2MASS Discoveries near the Galactic Plane: A Spiral Galaxy and Two Globular Clusters. The Astronomical Journal, Volume 120, Issue 4, pp. 1876-1883 (10/2000). [ADS: 2000AJ....120.1876H] - [Preprint] Discovery announce of two new globulars, 2MASS-GC01 and 2MASS-GC02.

Henry Kobulnicky, B.L. Babler, T.M. Bania, R.A. Benjamin, B.A. Buckalew, R. Canterna, E. Churchwell, D. Clemens, M. Cohen, J.M. Darnel, J.M. Dickey, R. Indebetouw, J.M. Jackson, A. Kutyrev, A.P. Marston, J.S. Mathis, M.R. Meade, E.P. Mercer, A.J. Monson, J.P. Norris, M.J. Pierce, R. Shah, J.R. Stauffer, S.R. Stolovy, B. Uzpen, C. Watson, B.A. Whitney, M.J. Wolff, and M.G. Wolfire, 2004. Newfound Star Cluster may be final Milky Way 'Fossil.' Spitzer Science Center News Release 2004-16. Discovery announce of the new globular GLIMPSE-C01.

S. Koposov, J.T.A. de Jong, H.-W. Rix, D.B. Zucker, N.W. Evans, G. Gilmore, M.J. Irwin, E.F. Bell, 2007. The discovery of two extremely low luminosity Milky Way globular clusters. Submitted to Astrophysical Journal. [Preprint: arXiv:0706.0019[astro-ph]] Discovery paper of Koposov 1 and Koposov 2.

S. Ortolani, E. Bica and B. Barbuy (2000). ESO 280-SC06: a new globular cluster in the Galaxy. Astronomy and Astrophysics, Vol. 361, pp. L57-L59 (September 2000). [ADS: 2000A&A...361L..57O] Discovery announce of the new globular, ESO 280-SC06.

S. Ortolani, E. Bica and B. Barbuy, 2006. AL 3 (BH 261): a new globular cluster in the Galaxy. Astrophysical Journal, Vol. 646, Issue 2, pp. L115-L118 (August 2006) [ADS: 2006ApJ...646L.115O] - [Preprint: astro-ph/0606718]. Discovery announce of the globular nature of AL-3.